Are you **Stressed?**

- Do you sometimes feel like you are running round and round but you just can't cope with life?
- Here is the solution: Journaling for Stress Release
- Includes Motivational Quotes to help you relax

Fiona MacKay

Praise for My Inspirational & Healing Journals

I have read so often that one should write out one's stress, as that in itself is a great help. I love having a journal just for that – and the quotes are so helpful when I'm stressed out.

Marnie Ritchards, Columbus, OH

This is wonderful! The journal and quotes are great, really great. But the list of stress-busters plus the list for me to create of what works best for me is pure inspiration. Wonderful Journal – everyone should have one!

Lorraine Camp, Surrey, UK

Well, I don't know if anyone has come up with a cure for stress yet, but this must come close. It is absolutely terrific. Quotes, stress relieving activities both yours and mine, a place to record what I want to find again – plus of course space to journal. Absolutely the best tool possible

Frances Gould, Honolulu, HI

My Healing Relaxation Journal is part of the "My Inspirational Journal" series, with more to follow.

Keeping you inspired!

My Healing Relaxation Journal

Release Stress

Create Calm

Copyright (c) 2014 by Fiona MacKay. All rights reserved.

No part of this publication may be reproduced, or transmitted in any form or by any means, electronic, mechanical, photocopying, recording, scanning or otherwise, except as permitted under International Copyright Laws without either the prior written permission of the author or authorization through payment of the appropriate per-copy fee.

Requests for permission should be addressed to Fiona MacKay at fionamackayjournals@gmail.com.

This publication is designed to provide inspiration and encouragement in regard to the subject matter covered. It is sold with the understanding that the author is not responsible for any reaction to, or action taken or not taken as a result of reading this material.

Copyright (c) 2014 by Fiona MacKay.

Before you agree to do anything that might add even the smallest amount of stress to your life, ask yourself:

"What is my truest intention?"

Give yourself time to let a YES resound within you.

When it is right, I guarantee that your entire body will feel it.

Oprah Winfrey

My Healing Relaxation Journal

Release Stress Create Calm

Table of Contents

Introduction	1
My Favorite De-Stressors	7
Suggested De-Stressor Activities	11
Quotes & Journaling Pages	18
Memory Jogger	
Dates to Remember	191

Introduction to
My Healing Relaxation Journal:
Release Stress Create Calm

Stress is a killer. We have heard that so often from so many places, and it is true.

But really, just knowing that solves nothing.

In fact, from my own perspective, just knowing that something I am doing involuntarily and don't know how to stop is killing me just adds to the stress that is killing me in the first place!

This journal is a result of my own search for something to help reduce my stress.

I don't handle stress at all well, so in the interests of a long and happy life, I had to do something to reduce it drastically. I don't live a high paced or high pressured lifestyle, but I manage get completely stressed out about things anyway.

So whether you live what would generally be recognized as being in a high stressed environment, or

My Inspirational Relaxation Journal: Release Stress Create Calm

whether you appear to the outside world to have a relatively calm existence but get stressed anyway, this journal is for you.

In my opinion it uses the very best de-stressing technique in the world plus I've added a few extras.

My solution to stress is to **journal**. And this journal is designed to encourage you to do so too in stressful times.

This journal has as its focus "stress release" and comes not only with motivational and stress-busting tips every time you turn the page, but it also has an extensive stress release ideas list to inspire you, and a place to write down all your own favorite stress relieving activities.

I suggest you journal first about what it stressing you out at this moment. Then secondly journal about what you can do to fix the situation or, if not, then how best reduce the stress.

Talk it out with yourself and often you may find that there is nothing to be stressed out about in the first place. Or you may well be in a busier than usual, more stressed situation where many people would be feeling stressed, in which case the same idea – talking it out with yourself in your journal - works beautifully.

Just sit down and unburden your poor little stressed out mind, heart and soul for as long as it takes to feel you've covered everything and got it all out there.

Once you've got all that out, you will probably be feeling better already.

Next start to journal about what will make things better.

What can you do to reduce the stress, or to feel less stressed about situations you can't change?

Or even just to write down how things really are, without the imaginings of your mind which make it seem worse when you just allow your thoughts to wander.

For me this two-step process works extremely well. I keep on journaling on the subject until the stress situation passes or is under control (in my mind as well as in reality.)

Here is the simple two-step process:

My Inspirational Relaxation Journal: Release Stress Create Calm

1. Journal to unburden yourself of how you feel, what your fears are and about what is upsetting you. Just pour it all out into your journal. Take as long as you want. The more complete this part, the easier it is to succeed with the second part.
2. Take a deep breath now it's all out there, and turn your mind to what can make things better. This may involve actual actions or it may more take place in your mind, or both. Changing your mindset can, depending on the situation, be just as effective as changing the situation.

Extra help, motivation and encouragement come with the quote you will find each time you turn the page. They are there to help you let go of that stress.

There is also a handy Memory Jogger Index at the back where you can record page numbers or dates of any entries, such as solutions to problems, or quotes that really speak to you, for easy retrieval.

Journaling is wonderful tool whether you are stressed or not. It is plain and simply one of the healthiest tools

My Inspirational Relaxation Journal: Release Stress Create Calm

available to keep your mind healthy, happy and focused.

And the Relaxation Journal adds to that benefit by focusing on helping you through the stressful times in your life, making them easier to bear and giving you back the feeling of being in control.

I encourage you to Journal your stress into oblivion. It works for me every time. I hope it works for you.

What things do you do, can you do that you know takes your mind off your stress?

Anything that releases you from worry and stress for even a few minutes belongs on your list of Favorite De-stressors (next page.)

Beyond this is a list of Suggested De-Stressor Activities for you to choose and mark whichever work best for you, or seem most appealing to try.

You may add them to your list here, or just highlight them on the original list.

Just keep adding your own to your list as you discover them.

My Inspirational Relaxation Journal: Release Stress Create Calm

When you're feeling particularly stressed, just go to these lists and choose something that appeals to you at that moment so relax you more.

My Inspirational Relaxation Journal: Release Stress Create Calm

My Favorite De-Stressors

My Inspirational Relaxation Journal:
Release Stress Create Calm

My Inspirational Relaxation Journal: Release Stress Create Calm

My Inspirational Relaxation Journal: Release Stress Create Calm

My Inspirational Relaxation Journal:
Release Stress Create Calm

Suggested De-Stressor Activities

1. ***Write in your journal and tell it how you really feel***
2. Take a Bath
3. Listen to music
4. Take a nap
5. Go to a body of water
6. Rest with our legs up on a wall
7. Reminisce about good times
8. Ask for a hug
9. In every difficulty look for an opportunity
10. Do some gentle stretches
11. Watch the clouds
12. Use visualization techniques and affirmations
13. Read old journals of happy times
14. Sit outside and enjoy the sounds
15. Burn some aromatherapy oils
16. Light a candle
17. Listen to a guided relaxation
18. Let out a sigh
19. Fly a kite
20. Watch the stars
21. Dance it out
22. Write a letter
23. Read a book

My Inspirational Relaxation Journal:
Release Stress Create Calm

24. Put on some music and dance
25. Sit in nature
26. Move twice as slowly
27. Take deep belly breaths
28. Meditate
29. Call a friend
30. Meander around town
31. Buy some flowers
32. Find a relaxing scent
33. Notice your body
34. Go for a run
35. Eat a meal in silence
36. Turn off electronics
37. Take a bike ride
38. Go to a part
39. Pet a furry creature
40. Create your own coffee break
41. View some art
42. Examine an everyday object with new eyes
43. Drive somewhere new
44. Climb a tree
45. Go to a farmers market
46. Forgive someone
47. Read or watch something funny
48. Do a random act of kindness
49. Color with crayons
50. Make some music
51. Let go of something
52. Paint on a surface other than paper

My Inspirational Relaxation Journal: Release Stress Create Calm

53. Write a quick poem
54. Read poetry
55. Give thanks
56. Talk about it – to someone else or to yourself in the mirror
57. Cry if you feel like it
58. Have a hot bath then go for a nap
59. Focus on what you **can** control
60. Smile for yourself, and give your smile to others
61. Pamper yourself with a manicure, wash your hair and spend time styling it in a new way
62. Compliment someone
63. Get involved in a cause your are passionate about
64. Take a dance class
65. Play with a puppy or a kitten
66. Make a list of things that make you happy
67. Turn off your phone
68. Take some "me time" right now
69. Remember – this too shall pass
70. Laugh
71. Step away from the situation and concentrate on something that makes you happy
72. Identify for yourself what you really want – on paper (in this journal?)
73. Get help – you don't have to do it all alone
74. Re-evaluate your priorities: what is really important right now
75. Run late. It happens to everyone

My Inspirational Relaxation Journal:
Release Stress Create Calm

76. Bake something that is a favorite: soothing aromas, familiar movements and delicious eating afterwards
77. Sing – even if you think you can't
78. Turn off the computer
79. Eat that cupcake
80. Let it go. The past if over, what's done is done
81. Say no\
82. Return a call or email tomorrow
83. Skip the gym unless you really WANT to go
84. Indulge in a guilty pleasure
85. Watch your favorite movie
86. Engage your visual senses in photographs, or paintings
87. Allow yourself to day dream for half an hour
88. Use scented candles
89. Eat dark chocolate cover almonds
90. Wear your most comfortable clothes
91. Have a massage

My Inspirational Relaxation Journal:
Release Stress Create Calm

Are you **Stressed?**

- Do you sometimes feel like you are running round and round but you just can't cope with life?
- Here is the solution: Journaling for Stress Release
- Includes Motivational Quotes to help you relax

Fiona MacKay

My Inspirational Relaxation Journal:
Release Stress Create Calm

My Inspirational Relaxation Journal:
Release Stress Create Calm

Start Journaling here....

The time to relax is when you don't have time for it.

Sydney J. Harris

Date

How much Relaxation did you achieve today:

●●●●● 5   ●●●● 4   ●●● 3   ●● 2

or - Tomorrow will be better

Happiness is a choice. You can choose to be happy. There's going to be stress in life, but it's your choice whether you let it affect you or not.

Valerie Bertinelli

Date

How much Relaxation did you achieve today:
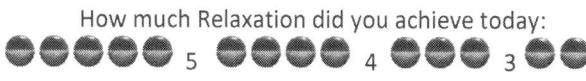

or - Tomorrow will be better

Your mind will answer most questions if you learn to relax and wait for the answer.

William S. Burroughs

Date

How much Relaxation did you achieve today:

🔴🔴🔴🔴🔴 5   🔴🔴🔴🔴 4   🔴🔴🔴 3   🔴🔴 2

or - Tomorrow will be better   🔴

The greatest weapon against stress is our ability to choose one thought over another.

William James

Date

How much Relaxation did you achieve today: 5   4   3   2

or - Tomorrow will be better

Nothing is permanent in this world – not even our troubles

Charlie Chaplin

Date

How much Relaxation did you achieve today:

⚫⚫⚫⚫⚫ 5   ⚫⚫⚫⚫ 4   ⚫⚫⚫ 3   ⚫⚫ 2

or - Tomorrow will be better   ⚫

It's not stress that kills us; it is our reaction to it.

Hans Selye

Date
_____

_____

_____

_____

_____

_____

_____

_____

_____

_____

_____

_____

_____

How much Relaxation did you achieve today:

●●●●● 5   ●●●● 4   ●●● 3   ●● 2

or - Tomorrow will be better   ●

There is no need to go to India or anywhere else to find peace. You will find that deep place of silence right in your room, your garden or even your bathtub.

Elisabeth Kubler-Ross

Date

How much Relaxation did you achieve today:

5 4 3 2

or - Tomorrow will be better

One of the best pieces of advice I ever got was from a horse master. He told me to go slow to go fast. I think that applies to everything in life. We live as though there aren't enough hours in the day but if we do each thing calmly and carefully we will get it done quicker and with much less stress.

Viggo Mortensen

Date

How much Relaxation did you achieve today:
●●●●● 5   ●●●●● 4   ●●●● 3   ●●● 2

or - Tomorrow will be better

The mark of a successful man is one that has spent an entire day on the bank of a river without feeling guilty about it.

Unknown

Date

How much Relaxation did you achieve today:
● ● ● ● ● ● 5   ● ● ● ● ● 4   ● ● ● ● 3   ● ● ● 2

or - Tomorrow will be better ●

Many of us feel stress and get overwhelmed not because we're taking on too much, but because we're taking on too little of what really strengthens us.

Marcus Buckingham

Date

How much Relaxation did you achieve today:

⬤⬤⬤⬤⬤ 5   ⬤⬤⬤⬤ 4   ⬤⬤⬤ 3   ⬤⬤ 2

or - Tomorrow will be better   ⬤

Like steam from a cup of hot tea that fogs our glasses, false urgency of matters at hand blurs our vision to the important things in the distance.

Terri Guillemets

Date

How much Relaxation did you achieve today:

5   4   3   2

or - Tomorrow will be better

Live in the moment, day by day, and don't stress about the future. People are so caught up in looking into the future, that they kind of lose what's in front of them.

Jenna Ushkowitz

Date

How much Relaxation did you achieve today:

⬤⬤⬤⬤⬤ 5   ⬤⬤⬤⬤ 4   ⬤⬤⬤ 3   ⬤⬤ 2

or - Tomorrow will be better   ⬤

Doing something that is productive is a great way to alleviate emotional stress.

Get your mind doing something that is productive.

Ziggy Marley

Date

How much Relaxation did you achieve today:
● ● ● ● ● 5 ● ● ● ● 4 ● ● ● 3 ● ● 2

or - Tomorrow will be better ●

Everything you do can be done better from a place of relaxation.

Stephen C. Paul

Date

How much Relaxation did you achieve today:

●●●●● 5   ●●●● 4   ●●● 3   ●● 2

or - Tomorrow will be better ●

The components of anxiety, stress, fear, and anger do not exist independently of you in the world.

They simply do not exist in the physical world, even though we talk about them as if they do.

Wayne Dyer

Date

How much Relaxation did you achieve today:

5 4 3 2

or - Tomorrow will be better

Softly and kindly remind yourself, "I cannot own anything." It is a valuable thought to keep in mind as you struggle to improve your financial picture, worry about investments and plan not to acquire more and more.

It is a universal principle which you are part of.

You must release everything when you truly awaken.

Are you letting your life go by in frustration and worry over not having enough? If so, relax and remember that you only get what you have for a short period of time. When you awaken you will see the folly of being attached to anything.

Wayne Dyer

Date

How much Relaxation did you achieve today:

or - Tomorrow will be better

We all enjoy pushing ourselves to accomplish our objectives.

But we don't need stress to get there.

Andrew Bernstein

Date

How much Relaxation did you achieve today:
●●●●● 5 ●●●● 4 ●●● 3 ●● 2

or - Tomorrow will be better ●

Who among us hasn't envied a cat's ability to ignore the cares of daily life and to relax completely?

Karen Brademeyer

Date

How much Relaxation did you achieve today:
⬤⬤⬤⬤⬤ 5   ⬤⬤⬤⬤ 4   ⬤⬤⬤ 3   ⬤⬤ 2

or - Tomorrow will be better ⬤

Stress is an important dragon to slay - or at least tame - in your life.

Marilu Henner

Date

How much Relaxation did you achieve today:
●●●●● 5 ●●●●● 4 ●●●● 3 ●● 2

or - Tomorrow will be better ●

Your mind will answer most questions if you learn to relax and wait for the answer.

William S. Burroughs

Date

How much Relaxation did you achieve today:

 5   4   3   2

or - Tomorrow will be better

There is more to life than increasing its speed.

Mohandas K. Gandhi

Date

How much Relaxation did you achieve today:

or - Tomorrow will be better

Don't fill your head with worries. There won't be room for anything else.

Unknown

Date

How much Relaxation did you achieve today:

or - Tomorrow will be better

How beautiful it is to do nothing, and then to rest afterward.

Spanish Proverb

Date

How much Relaxation did you achieve today:
⬤⬤⬤⬤⬤ 5   ⬤⬤⬤⬤ 4   ⬤⬤⬤ 3   ⬤⬤ 2

or - Tomorrow will be better ⬤

I am in charge of how I feel and today I am choosing happiness.

Unknown

Date

How much Relaxation did you achieve today:
5 4 3 2
or - Tomorrow will be better

Don't underestimate the value of Doing Nothing, of just going along, listening to all the things you can't hear, and not bothering.

Pooh's Little Instruction Book, inspired by A.A. Milne

Date

How much Relaxation did you achieve today:
⬤⬤⬤⬤⬤ 5 ⬤⬤⬤⬤ 4 ⬤⬤⬤ 3 ⬤⬤ 2

or - Tomorrow will be better ⬤

Do what you can.

With what you have.

Where you are.

Theodore Roosevelt

 Date

How much Relaxation did you achieve today:

5 4 3 2

or - Tomorrow will be better

When you are dealing with stress, the problem may not be the stressful situation, as much as the effort to avoid that situation and the feelings it arouses.

Ted. A. Grossbart

Date

How much Relaxation did you achieve today:
⬤⬤⬤⬤⬤ 5   ⬤⬤⬤⬤ 4   ⬤⬤⬤ 3   ⬤⬤ 2

or - Tomorrow will be better   ⬤

Strength doesn't come from what you can do.
It comes from overcoming the things you once thought you couldn't do.

Unknown

Date

How much Relaxation did you achieve today:

🌑🌑🌑🌑🌑 5   🌑🌑🌑🌑 4   🌑🌑🌑 3   🌑🌑 2

or - Tomorrow will be better 🌑

Worry pretends to be necessary but it serves no useful purpose.

Unknown

Date

How much Relaxation did you achieve today:
⬤⬤⬤⬤⬤ 5   ⬤⬤⬤⬤ 4   ⬤⬤⬤ 3   ⬤⬤ 2

or - Tomorrow will be better

Good things are going to happen.

Unknown

Date

How much Relaxation did you achieve today:
●●●●● 5 ●●●●● 4 ●●●● 3 ●●● 2

or - Tomorrow will be better ●

What we think, we become.

Buddha

(Think Stress, become stressed.)

Date

How much Relaxation did you achieve today:
⬤⬤⬤⬤⬤ 5 ⬤⬤⬤⬤ 4 ⬤⬤⬤ 3 ⬤⬤ 2

or - Tomorrow will be better ⬤

She believed she could,
So she did.

Unknown

Date

How much Relaxation did you achieve today:
⚫⚫⚫⚫⚫ 5 ⚫⚫⚫⚫ 4 ⚫⚫⚫ 3 ⚫⚫ 2

or - Tomorrow will be better ⚫

In times of great stress or adversity, it's always best to keep busy, to plow your anger and your energy into something positive.

Lee Iacocca

Date

How much Relaxation did you achieve today:
⚫⚫⚫⚫⚫ 5 ⚫⚫⚫⚫ 4 ⚫⚫⚫ 3 ⚫⚫ 2

or - Tomorrow will be better ⚫

Be OK with where you are, even if you know you want to change.

Unknown

Date

How much Relaxation did you achieve today:

●●●●● 5   ●●●● 4   ●●● 3   ●● 2

or - Tomorrow will be better ●

The truth is that stress doesn't come from your boss, your kids, your spouse, traffic jams, health challenges, or other circumstances.

It comes from your thoughts about these circumstances.

Andrew Bernstein

Date

How much Relaxation did you achieve today:
5 4 3 2

or - Tomorrow will be better

Out of clutter find simplicity,

from discord find harmony,

in the middle of difficulty lies opportunity.

Albert Einstein

Date

How much Relaxation did you achieve today:
 5 　 4 　 3 　 2

or - Tomorrow will be better

Adopting the right attitude can convert a negative stress into a positive one.

Hans Selye

Date

How much Relaxation did you achieve today:
🔴🔴🔴🔴🔴 5 🔴🔴🔴🔴 4 🔴🔴🔴 3 🔴🔴 2

or - Tomorrow will be better 🔴

Sometimes all you need is a good cup of tea.

Unknown

(but almost certainly British!)

Date

How much Relaxation did you achieve today:

⬤⬤⬤⬤⬤ 5   ⬤⬤⬤⬤ 4   ⬤⬤⬤ 3   ⬤⬤ 2

or - Tomorrow will be better   ⬤

As far as having peace within myself, the one way I can do that is forgiving the people who have done wrong to me.

It causes more stress to build up anger.

Peace is more productive.

Rodney King

Date

How much Relaxation did you achieve today:

5   4   3   2

or - Tomorrow will be better

A diamond is just a piece of charcoal that handles stress exceptionally well.

Unknown

Date _____

_____

_____

_____

_____

_____

_____

_____

_____

_____

_____

_____

How much Relaxation did you achieve today:

●●●●● 5 ●●●● 4 ●●● 3 ●● 2

or - Tomorrow will be better ●

We get caught up in all the stress - 'Got to do this, is this the right thing for me to do?' - but what about the thing you want to do?

That's what'll keep you young. It's empowering, not becoming a prisoner of some other person's idea of what you should be.

Matt Dillon

Date

How much Relaxation did you achieve today:

or - Tomorrow will be better

No day is so back it can't be fixed with a nap.

Unknown

Date

_____

_____

_____

_____

_____

_____

_____

_____

_____

_____

_____

_____

How much Relaxation did you achieve today:

●●●●● 5   ●●●● 4   ●●● 3   ●● 2

or - Tomorrow will be better

What's taking place during stress is actually much simpler than a transaction between stressful life events and you.

There aren't two parties involved in stress.

There is only one - your own mind.

Andrew Bernstein

Date

How much Relaxation did you achieve today:

🌑🌑🌑🌑🌑 5   🌑🌑🌑🌑 4   🌑🌑🌑 3   🌑🌑 2

or - Tomorrow will be better 🌑

The best six doctors anywhere are:

- Sunshine
- Water
- Rest
- Air
- Exercise
- Diet

Wayne Fields

(and you don't need a health care plan to afford them.)

Date

How much Relaxation did you achieve today:

⬤⬤⬤⬤⬤ 5   ⬤⬤⬤⬤ 4   ⬤⬤⬤ 3   ⬤⬤ 2

or - Tomorrow will be better ⬤

"There must be quite a few things that a hot bath won't cure, but I don't know many of them."

Sylvia Plath

Date

How much Relaxation did you achieve today:

🔴🔴🔴🔴🔴 5   🔴🔴🔴🔴 4   🔴🔴🔴 3   🔴🔴 2

or - Tomorrow will be better

10 to Zen

1. Let go of comparing
2. Let go of competing
3. Let go of judgments
4. Let go of anger
5. Let go of regrets
6. Let go of worrying
7. Let go of blame
8. Let go of guilt
9. Let go of fear
10. Have a proper belly laugh at least once a day (especially if it's about your inability to let go of any of all of the above)

Unknown

Date

How much Relaxation did you achieve today:
●●●●● 5 ●●●● 4 ●●● 3 ●● 2

or - Tomorrow will be better ●

If you are distressed by anything external, the pain is not due to the thing itself, but to your estimate of it; and this you have the power to revoke at any moment.

Marcus Aurelius

Date

How much Relaxation did you achieve today:
●●●●● 5 ●●●● 4 ●●● 3 ●● 2

or - Tomorrow will be better ●

How to Just Be

1. Feel yourself breathing
2. Feel the light pressure of your heart beating against your ribcage
3. Feel the empty space behind your eyeballs
4. Feel you as just you being you and being ok with it.

Yimo Sakugawa

Date

How much Relaxation did you achieve today:

⬤⬤⬤⬤⬤ 5   ⬤⬤⬤⬤ 4   ⬤⬤⬤ 3   ⬤⬤ 2

or - Tomorrow will be better   ⬤

God didn't do it all in one day.
What makes me think I can?

Unknown

Date

How much Relaxation did you achieve today:

or - Tomorrow will be better

I will accept things I cannot change.

Unknown

Date

How much Relaxation did you achieve today:

or - Tomorrow will be better

Slow down and everything you are chasing will come around and catch you.

John De Paola

Date

How much Relaxation did you achieve today:

 5 ●●●●● 4 ●●●● 3 ●● 2

or - Tomorrow will be better

If "Plan A" didn't work, the alphabet has 25 more letters you can use.

Stay cool.

Unknown

Date

How much Relaxation did you achieve today:

or - Tomorrow will be better

If people concentrated on the really important things in life, there'd be a shortage of fishing poles.

Doug Larson

Date

_____

_____

_____

_____

_____

_____

_____

_____

_____

_____

_____

_____

How much Relaxation did you achieve today:

●●●●● 5   ●●●●● 4   ●●●● 3   ●●● 2

or - Tomorrow will be better

Recharge

1. No emailing after work hours
2. Eat for energy not for comfort
3. Read in the tub
4. Schedule a hot yoga class
5. Take a real lunch break
6. Laugh more
7. Go to be by 11 pm
8. Sip green tea (with pomegranate)
9. Hug someone every day
10. Revel in success before moving on

                        Unknown

Date

How much Relaxation did you achieve today:
🌑🌑🌑🌑🌑 5   🌑🌑🌑🌑 4   🌑🌑🌑 3   🌑🌑 2

or - Tomorrow will be better

"Stressed" is "Desserts" spelled backwards.

Co-incidence? I think not!

Unknown

Date

How much Relaxation did you achieve today:
5 4 3 2

or - Tomorrow will be better

Most humans are never fully present in the now, because unconsciously they believe that the next moment must be more important than this one.

But then you miss your whole life, which is never NOT now.

And that's a revelation for some people: to realize that your life is only ever now.

Eckhart Tolle

Date

How much Relaxation did you achieve today:
⚫⚫⚫⚫⚫ 5 ⚫⚫⚫⚫ 4 ⚫⚫⚫ 3 ⚫⚫ 2

or - Tomorrow will be better ⚫

Next time you're stressed, take a step back, inhale and laugh.

Remember who you are and why you're here. You're never given anything in this world that you can't handle.

Be strong, be flexible, love yourself, and love others.

Always remember, just keep moving forwards.

Unknown

Date

How much Relaxation did you achieve today:
●●●●● 5 ●●●● 4 ●●● 3 ●● 2

or - Tomorrow will be better

Close your eyes,
clear your heart,
let it go.

Unknown

Date

How much Relaxation did you achieve today:

or - Tomorrow will be better

Always remember you are braver than you believe, stronger than you seem, and smarter than you think.

Unknown

Date

How much Relaxation did you achieve today:
5   4   3   2

or - Tomorrow will be better

A silent hug means a thousand words to the unhappy heart.

Unknown

Date

How much Relaxation did you achieve today:

⬤⬤⬤⬤⬤ 5 ⬤⬤⬤⬤ 4 ⬤⬤⬤ 3 ⬤⬤ 2

or - Tomorrow will be better ⬤

A woman under stress is not immediately concerned with finding solutions to her problems but rather seeks relief by expressing herself and being understood.

John Gray

Date

How much Relaxation did you achieve today:

or - Tomorrow will be better

There cannot be a stressful crisis next week.

My schedule is already full.

Henry Kissinger

Date

How much Relaxation did you achieve today:

 5   4   3   2

or - Tomorrow will be better

All the suffering and stress comes from not realizing you already are what you are looking for.

Jon Kabat-Zinn

Date

How much Relaxation did you achieve today:
5   4   3   2

or - Tomorrow will be better

We live in times of high stress. Messages that are simple, messages that are inspiring, messages that are life-affirming are a welcome break from our real lives.

Simon Sinek

Date

How much Relaxation did you achieve today:

⬤⬤⬤⬤⬤ 5   ⬤⬤⬤⬤ 4   ⬤⬤⬤ 3   ⬤⬤ 2

or - Tomorrow will be better ⬤

Stress is a byproduct of subconscious beliefs you have about the world. You can't choose not to believe something. You believe it because you think it's true. To eliminate stress, you must learn to challenge these beliefs so that you see them differently.

Andrew Bernstein

Date

How much Relaxation did you achieve today:

or - Tomorrow will be better

The time to relax is when you don't have time for it.

Sydney J. Harris

Date

How much Relaxation did you achieve today:
⬤⬤⬤⬤⬤ 5 ⬤⬤⬤⬤ 4 ⬤⬤⬤ 3 ⬤⬤ 2

or - Tomorrow will be better

Is everything as urgent as your stress would imply?

Carrie Latet

Date
_____

How much Relaxation did you achieve today:

🌑🌑🌑🌑🌑 5   🌑🌑🌑🌑 4   🌑🌑🌑 3   🌑🌑 2

or - Tomorrow will be better   🌑

Tension is who you think you should be.

Relaxation is who you are.

Chinese Proverb

Date

How much Relaxation did you achieve today:

5 4 3 2

or - Tomorrow will be better

I try to take one day at a time, but sometimes several days attack me at once.

Jennifer Yane

Date

How much Relaxation did you achieve today:

⬤⬤⬤⬤⬤ 5 ⬤⬤⬤⬤ 4 ⬤⬤⬤ 3 ⬤⬤ 2

or - Tomorrow will be better

The greatest weapon against stress is our ability to choose one thought over another.

William James

Date

How much Relaxation did you achieve today:

●●●●● 5 ●●●● 4 ●●● 3 ●● 2

or - Tomorrow will be better

God will never give you anything you can't handle, so don't stress.

Kelly Clarkson

Date

How much Relaxation did you achieve today:

⬤⬤⬤⬤⬤ 5   ⬤⬤⬤⬤ 4   ⬤⬤⬤ 3   ⬤⬤ 2

or - Tomorrow will be better   ⬤

Remember that stress doesn't come from what's going on in your life.

It comes from your thoughts about what's going on in your life.

Andrew Bernstein

Date

How much Relaxation did you achieve today:
5 4 3 2

or - Tomorrow will be better

Laughter is a core workout.

I feed the soul, makes life better, has no calories, it's free and contagious.

Have you indulged today?

Unknown

Date

How much Relaxation did you achieve today: 5 4 3 2

or - Tomorrow will be better

Sometimes when people are under stress, they hate to think, and it's the time when they most need to think.

William J. Clinton

Date

How much Relaxation did you achieve today:

⬤⬤⬤⬤⬤ 5   ⬤⬤⬤⬤ 4   ⬤⬤⬤ 3   ⬤⬤ 2

or - Tomorrow will be better

Don't use your energy to worry.

Use your energy to believe.

Unknown

Date

How much Relaxation did you achieve today:
🌑🌑🌑🌑🌑 5   🌑🌑🌑🌑 4   🌑🌑🌑 3   🌑🌑 2

or - Tomorrow will be better 🌑

If you're successful and stressed out, you're succeeding in spite of your stress, not because of it.

Andrew Bernstein

Date

How much Relaxation did you achieve today:

5   4   3   2

or - Tomorrow will be better

Drop the idea that you are Atlas, carrying the world on your shoulders.

The world would go n even without you.

Don't take yourself so seriously.

Norman Vincent Peale

Date

How much Relaxation did you achieve today:

or - Tomorrow will be better

It makes no sense to worry about things you have no control over because there's nothing you can do about them, and why worry about things you do control?

The activity of worrying keeps you immobilized.

Wayne Dyer

Date

How much Relaxation did you achieve today:

or - Tomorrow will be better

You have enough.

You do enough.

You are enough.

Relax.

Unknown

Date

How much Relaxation did you achieve today:

or - Tomorrow will be better

How we perceive a situation and how we react to it is the basis of our stress.

If you focus on the negative in any situation, you can expect high stress levels.

However, if you try and see the good in the situation, your stress levels will greatly diminish.

Catherine Pulsifer

Date

How much Relaxation did you achieve today:

●●●●● 5   ●●●● 4   ●●● 3   ●● 2

or - Tomorrow will be better

You've heard of FIGHT and FLIGHT instincts?

Well, there's also the popular BITE instinct.

During stressful times you want to bite, to eat lots of food.

During these times choose the wiser WRITE instinct.

Write out your feelings in your journal instead.

Unknown

Date

How much Relaxation did you achieve today:
⬤⬤⬤⬤⬤ 5   ⬤⬤⬤⬤ 4   ⬤⬤⬤ 3   ⬤⬤ 2

or - Tomorrow will be better ⬤

Stress is an ignorant state.

It believes that everything is an emergency.

Natalie Goldberg

Date

___

How much Relaxation did you achieve today:

⬤⬤⬤⬤⬤ 5 ⬤⬤⬤⬤ 4 ⬤⬤⬤ 3 ⬤⬤ 2

or - Tomorrow will be better ⬤

The Secret to a Good Life is to never stop...

- Smiling
- Dreaming
- Loving
- Hugging
- Holding
- Searching
- Thanking
- Feeling
- Learning
- Playing
- Laughing
- thinking
- wishing
- forgiving
- healing
- expressing
- appreciating
- believing
- cherishing
- creating
- hoping
- living

Date

How much Relaxation did you achieve today:
5   4   3   2

or - Tomorrow will be better

Releasing the pressure, it's good for the teapot and the water.

Try it sometime.

Jeb Dickerson

Date

How much Relaxation did you achieve today:

🌑🌑🌑🌑🌑 5   🌑🌑🌑🌑 4   🌑🌑🌑 3   🌑🌑 2

or - Tomorrow will be better   🌑

Find a beautiful place and get lost

Unknown

Date

How much Relaxation did you achieve today:

or - Tomorrow will be better

Tears are good. What flows is alive.

Crying is like a thundershower for the soul. The air feels so wonderful after the rain.

Don't think too much. Breathe.

Don't be harsh or demanding on yourself.

Just experience your feelings and know that your tears are announcing change in your life.

Change is coming; like a summer rain - to wash away your pain. Have faith that things are getting better.

Bryant McGill

Date

How much Relaxation did you achieve today:
 5    4    3    2

or - Tomorrow will be better

My Healing Relaxation Journal:
Release Stress Create Calm

My Healing Relaxation Journal:
Release Stress Create Calm

Memory Jogger

Dates to Remember

My Healing Relaxation Journal:
Release Stress Create Calm

Memory Jogger Dates to Remember

Date/Page   Quote ☐   Journal Entry ☐

Notes:

Date/Page   Quote ☐   Journal Entry ☐

Notes:

Date/Page   Quote ☐   Journal Entry ☐

Notes:

Date/Page   Quote ☐   Journal Entry ☐

Notes:

Date/Page   Quote ☐   Journal Entry ☐

Notes:

Date/Page   Quote ☐   Journal Entry ☐

Notes:

My Healing Relaxation Journal:
Release Stress Create Calm

Memory Jogger Dates to Remember

Date/Page   Quote ☐   Journal Entry ☐

Notes:

Date/Page   Quote ☐   Journal Entry ☐

Notes:

Date/Page   Quote ☐   Journal Entry ☐

Notes:

Date/Page   Quote ☐   Journal Entry ☐

Notes:

Date/Page   Quote ☐   Journal Entry ☐

Notes:

Date/Page   Quote ☐   Journal Entry ☐

Notes:

My Healing Relaxation Journal:
Release Stress Create Calm

Memory Jogger Dates to Remember

Date/Page   Quote ☐   Journal Entry ☐

Notes:

Date/Page   Quote ☐   Journal Entry ☐

Notes:

Date/Page   Quote ☐   Journal Entry ☐

Notes:

Date/Page   Quote ☐   Journal Entry ☐

Notes:

Date/Page   Quote ☐   Journal Entry ☐

Notes:

Date/Page   Quote ☐   Journal Entry ☐

Notes:

My Healing Relaxation Journal:
Release Stress Create Calm

Memory Jogger Dates to Remember

Date/Page　　　　　Quote ☐　Journal Entry ☐

Notes:

Date/Page　　　　　Quote ☐　Journal Entry ☐

Notes:

Date/Page　　　　　Quote ☐　Journal Entry ☐

Notes:

Date/Page　　　　　Quote ☐　Journal Entry ☐

Notes:

Date/Page　　　　　Quote ☐　Journal Entry ☐

Notes:

Date/Page　　　　　Quote ☐　Journal Entry ☐

Notes:

My Healing Relaxation Journal:
Release Stress Create Calm

Memory Jogger Dates to Remember

Date/Page   Quote ☐   Journal Entry ☐

Notes: _____

Date/Page   Quote ☐   Journal Entry ☐

Notes: _____

Date/Page   Quote ☐   Journal Entry ☐

Notes: _____

Date/Page   Quote ☐   Journal Entry ☐

Notes: _____

Date/Page   Quote ☐   Journal Entry ☐

Notes: _____

Date/Page   Quote ☐   Journal Entry ☐

Notes: _____

My Healing Relaxation Journal:
Release Stress Create Calm

Memory Jogger Dates to Remember

Date/Page   Quote ☐   Journal Entry ☐

Notes: _____

Date/Page   Quote ☐   Journal Entry ☐

Notes: _____

Date/Page   Quote ☐   Journal Entry ☐

Notes: _____

Date/Page   Quote ☐   Journal Entry ☐

Notes: _____

Date/Page   Quote ☐   Journal Entry ☐

Notes: _____

Date/Page   Quote ☐   Journal Entry ☐

Notes: _____

My Healing Relaxation Journal:
Release Stress Create Calm

Memory Jogger Dates to Remember

Date/Page   Quote ☐   Journal Entry ☐

Notes:

Date/Page   Quote ☐   Journal Entry ☐

Notes:

Date/Page   Quote ☐   Journal Entry ☐

Notes:

Date/Page   Quote ☐   Journal Entry ☐

Notes:

Date/Page   Quote ☐   Journal Entry ☐

Notes:

Date/Page   Quote ☐   Journal Entry ☐

Notes:

My Healing Relaxation Journal:
Release Stress Create Calm

Memory Jogger Dates to Remember

Date/Page   Quote ☐   Journal Entry ☐

Notes: _____

Date/Page   Quote ☐   Journal Entry ☐

Notes: _____

Date/Page   Quote ☐   Journal Entry ☐

Notes: _____

Date/Page   Quote ☐   Journal Entry ☐

Notes: _____

Date/Page   Quote ☐   Journal Entry ☐

Notes: _____

Date/Page   Quote ☐   Journal Entry ☐

Notes: _____

My Healing Relaxation Journal:
Release Stress Create Calm

My Healing Relaxation Journal:
Release Stress Create Calm

About the Author:

Fiona MacKay is a life/career coach and personality expert who uses the tool of journaling both with clients and for herself.

She has journaled for most of her life, and found it extremely helpful as a tool for motivation, creativity and generally keeping her life on an even keel.

She has developed her Inspirational & Healing Journals to help others maximize on the benefits of writing from the heart on a regular basis. Fiona totally believes that this is a tool to improve life, better relationships and generally enjoy all that life has to offer.

Fiona spends her time between the Pacific West Coast and various parts of the British Isles.

You can contact Fiona at fionamackayjournals@gmail.com or through her website as www.myinspirationaljournals.com

Made in the USA
Lexington, KY
13 January 2018